The Great Path

The Great Path

The Ancient Wisdom and Life-Changing Secrets of the Tao Te Ching

Kevin M. Thomas

THE GREAT PATH
The Ancient Wisdom and Life-Changing
Secrets of the Tao Te Ching
Kevin M. Thomas

KETNA Publishing
P.O. Box 90861 Burton, Michigan, 48509

Copyright © 2018 by Kevin M. Thomas

All rights reserved. No part of this book may be reproduced or transmitted in any form or by any means, electronic or mechanical, including photocopying, recording, or by any storage or retrieval system without permission in writing from copyright author.

For more information, address to KETNA Publishing
P.O. Box 90861, Burton, Michigan, 48509

First KETNA Printing Edition 2018

Cover Design By: 99Designs
Book Design By: Medlar Publishing Solutions Pvt Ltd., India
Proofreading By: Kelly Bixler and Sean Burns
of www.thewriteproofreader.com

is a registered trademark of KETNA Publishing

Printed in the USA

Library of Congress Control Number: 2017917734
ISBN: 978-0-9963874-6-0 (soft cover)
ISBN: 978-0-9963874-7-7 (hard cover)
ISBN: 978-0-9963874-8-4 (ebook)

Dedication

This book is dedicated to those seeking the right path; may they always be guided by God's wisdom. It is also dedicated to my dad, Grover, now embarking on a new journey in heaven, and to my mother, June, bravely fighting on in his absence. To my children—Isiah, Caroline, Kimberly, and Cheyenne—may they someday know all truth. Finally, to my fictional inspiration, Andy Dufresne, who said, "Hope is a good thing—maybe the best of things—and no good thing ever dies." So true, and so I go on, sharing and hoping, always seeking the right path.

Acknowledgments

Without God, I am nothing, and this book isn't written. Without Him, I have no vision or life or grace or mercy or future. Without Him and His miracles so great, perhaps many people wouldn't be able to see His wondrous ways. However, because of Him, I share His love, peace, compassion, and kindness for all humanity, hoping that they will ultimately seek His grace and love, and ultimately, His great path.

Next, I want to thank my dad. Over time, I was his son, his friend, and his caregiver until the circle of life essentially made him my son before we gently laid him to rest. May you forever rest with the angels, Dad.

To my brave and brokenhearted mother: Like myself, she will never be the same, but is slowly developing a new path surrounded by the music my dad loved.

To my children, Isiah, Caroline, Kimberly and Cheyenne: Sometimes life is not fair, but eventually, overall truth, compassion, and kindness win out. The fight is just beginning.

To Erik, my friend and brother: You are the most multitalented person I know with many accolades, and yet you would never know it because humbleness is among your greatest strengths. P.S. Where is my Grass-Pike Fishing Championship Trophy?

To Robin and Barb: You are both inspirational and spiritual rocks.

To the rest of my family and friends that are truly supportive souls: I thank you, and you know who you are.

Finally, to my fictional but inspirational characters, Andy Dufresne and Red: "Get busy living or get busy dying."

Table of Contents

Introduction . . . . *xii*
History of the Tao Te Ching . . . . *xv*
What is the Tao Te Ching? . . . . *xvii*

Chapter One 1
Chapter Two 2
Chapter Three 3
Chapter Four 4
Chapter Five 5
Chapter Six 6
Chapter Seven 7
Chapter Eight 8
Chapter Nine 9
Chapter Ten 10
Chapter Eleven 11
Chapter Twelve 12
Chapter Thirteen 13
Chapter Fourteen 14
Chapter Fifteen 15

Chapter Sixteen. 16
Chapter Seventeen. 17
Chapter Eighteen 18
Chapter Nineteen 19
Chapter Twenty. 20
Chapter Twenty-One. 21
Chapter Twenty-Two. 22
Chapter Twenty-Three. 23
Chapter Twenty-Four 24
Chapter Twenty-Five. 25
Chapter Twenty-Six. 26
Chapter Twenty-Seven. 27
Chapter Twenty-Eight. 28
Chapter Twenty-Nine 29
Chapter Thirty 30
Chapter Thirty-One 31
Chapter Thirty-Two 32
Chapter Thirty-Three 33
Chapter Thirty-Four 34
Chapter Thirty-Five. 35
Chapter Thirty-Six 36
Chapter Thirty-Seven 37
Chapter Thirty-Eight. 38

Chapter Thirty-Nine 39
Chapter Forty 40
Chapter Forty-One 41
Chapter Forty-Two 42
Chapter Forty-Three 43
Chapter Forty-Four 44
Chapter Forty-Five 45
Chapter Forty-Six 46
Chapter Forty-Seven 47
Chapter Forty-Eight 48
Chapter Forty-Nine 49
Chapter Fifty 50
Chapter Fifty-One 51
Chapter Fifty-Two 52
Chapter Fifty-Three 53
Chapter Fifty-Four 54
Chapter Fifty-Five 55
Chapter Fifty-Six 56
Chapter Fifty-Seven 57
Chapter Fifty-Eight 58
Chapter Fifty-Nine 59
Chapter Sixty 60
Chapter Sixty-One 61

Chapter Sixty-Two 62
Chapter Sixty-Three 63
Chapter Sixty-Four 64
Chapter Sixty-Five. 65
Chapter Sixty-Six 66
Chapter Sixty-Seven 67
Chapter Sixty-Eight. 68
Chapter Sixty-Nine 69
Chapter Seventy 70
Chapter Seventy-One 71
Chapter Seventy-Two 72
Chapter Seventy-Three 73
Chapter Seventy-Four 74
Chapter Seventy-Five 75
Chapter Seventy-Six 76
Chapter Seventy-Seven 77
Chapter Seventy-Eight 78
Chapter Seventy-Nine. 79
Chapter Eighty 80
Chapter Eighty-One 81

About the Author *82*
The Great Path. *83*

Introduction

Welcome aboard. I am happy to introduce to you *The Great Path*, which was written as a follow-up to my previous book, *Tao Te Ching De-Coded*. Now, you might be asking why I did another book on the *Tao Te Ching*. Well, as time went by, I was getting good feedback from others on my previous work, and soon found that even though the *Tao Te Ching* offered a basic, English version, people I talked to were clamoring for a more modern interpretation of this great classic—a straightforward version that was more applicable to their lives.

While *Tao Te Ching De-Coded* is a short, simplified version of great wisdom, translated directly, it can still seem vague and indirect to some, and in some places require reading between the lines. This was great for some people who prefer to come to their own conclusions over time. Of course, the original text was written hundreds of years ago to be intentionally vague to make people think, which of course, resulted in multiple interpretations.

However, I soon realized that another level of understanding is important—one that gives out a few more clues, but still helps people think and then find their own way. Apparently, it is a book worth reading, as the *Tao Te Ching* has been translated countless times in the Far East and over 250 times in Western languages with English, French, and German translations leading the way.

The impact of the *Tao Te Ching* has been far-reaching, as it is not only the basis of Chinese religion and philosophy, but a major influence on Confucianism and Buddhism that remains a deep source of inspiration for millions around the world. Like the Bible, it gives hope to those on the wrong path.

Speaking of the Bible, let me reach out to Christians because I am one, though this message pertains to other religious followers around the world as well. After I wrote *Tao Te Ching De-Coded*, I began to get some pushback from people who claimed to be Christian followers. So let me say this: God wants us to find as much common ground as possible with our fellow man and not create divisions. While this is a part of the religion that the Chinese follow, it certainly can be seen in a different way to those who follow Christianity. Isn't it wise to follow intelligent advice as long as it does not usurp or undermine what the Bible says for true followers, just like a concordance or a popular pastor writing a book to guide us?

It is the mature Christian who looks at the *Tao Te Ching* and says, "How can this help me? Where does this fit in?" While the immature Christian might say, "I don't care what it says; it is not for me." However, consider the wisdom of some Christian missionaries who compared some verses favorably with the New Testament and its wisdom. In the end, this is what this book is all about: bringing people together rather than causing hateful divisions, finding common ground, and making the world a better place where God is exalted with love.

History of the *Tao Te Ching*

The *Tao Te Ching* is thought to have been written around 600 BCE by a man named Laozi, who was also known as Lao Tzu, or "Old Master." Discoveries in the last century have shed new light on these famous works. For instance, in the 1920s and 1930s, explorer Marc Aurel Stein found several *Tao Te Ching* manuscripts that date back to 270 AD. In 1973, archaeologists found a group of books dating back to 168 BC that reverses the order of the book, putting the *Te Ching* first, and the *Tao Ching* second. Most modern translations have the *Tao Ching* (Chapters 1–37) coming first, and the *Te Ching* (Chapters 38–81) finishing the text. However, this discovery in 1973 suggests that the order could be reversed. Then, in 1993, the alleged oldest version of the text was found to be written on bamboo tablets. While most modern versions have five thousand characters, the discovery in 1993 revealed thirteen thousand characters, with two thousand of them directly related to the *Tao Te Ching*. So the mysteries, translations, and interpretations of the *Tao Te Ching* continue to unfold.

What is the *Tao Te Ching*?

The *Tao Te Ching*, which is also called the Daodejing or DaoDeJing, is classical Chinese text and considered one of the most important religious and philosophical works in the world of Taoism. It provides a key source of inspiration for millions of people around the world. The interpretation of the passages is virtually limitless, often covering wise decisions one should make or a wise path to take in a complicated world. The wisdom set forth in the book is often attained by gaining knowledge, humility, and experience, or by using many other tools or advice that the text has offered and passed down for hundreds of years.

For further understanding, the "Tao" or "Dao" basically means "The Way" or "The Way in the Universe." "Te" breaks down to mean "virtue, moral character, and even a deep inner strength or fortitude." "Ching" means a "great book." So we could say that the *Tao Te Ching* means "The Great Way to Inner Strength and Virtue" or "The Classical Book of Moral Virtue from the Universe."

Regardless, the *Tao Te Ching* is an excellent adjunct to making ourselves a better person and citizen, which, in turn, creates a better world.

Chapter One

In the beginning, there was God ruling over heaven and Earth. Many have desired to reach heaven and meet the unseen God. However, to accomplish this, a person must follow the greatest spiritual path so they can have eternal life. So it comes down to free will and our choices. On our earthly path, we must make the choice between following what is good and what is evil. What is good, and what is evil? Listen: If you follow and know what God wants for you, you are on the right and great path. The right path begins with knowing what God wants for you.

Chapter Two

To reach our ultimate destination of being with God in heaven, we must live without desire, called "wu-wei." It also means that at times, we must adjust our course to stay on the path that God has chosen for us. Yes, there will be a blending of hard times and joyous times along the way, but this mixture of hardness and softness helps develop us into the person God wants us to be. So let's not judge outer appearances, but rather let us treat others with compassion, for God sets before all of us our own path to follow that will honor Him.

Chapter Three

The first thing we must do to follow the path is to develop humbleness in ourselves. Let's not brag about what we have or what we have done, which only brings envy from others. There is no need to excessively praise some and not others, which brings jealousy by the appearance of playing favorites. Let us treat all people with love and respect, even when they can do little for us. To get people to follow you on the path, earn their trust, and don't show off. In the end, inspire people with good treatment. Feed them, let them measure up, strengthen them, and get them to relax. This will ensure that you won't have to fear people scheming against you. Why? It's because you have showed compassion.

Chapter Four

The right path is fruitful and full of wisdom. Its inspiration and guidance gives you all the tools needed to keep heading in the right direction. This great path is also a treasure trove of knowledge for yourself and to share with others. So when we apply the gifts of the great path, it leads to overwhelming love, compassion, and togetherness.

Chapter Five

When you follow the great and right path on Earth, the journey is guided by God and heaven above. It almost becomes a parallel journey of protection. You may have free will, but it is a blend of Earth and heaven as God guides your footsteps. It is a very real journey, not one to talk about or imagine in our minds. It must be experienced. So be open to the completeness of the oath, and it will lift you.

Chapter Six

When God created Earth, the rules of nature were also put forth. Some have also called them the rules of "mother earth" or "spirit valley." These laws of nature include the functioning plants, herbs, flowers, animals, and all their offspring. It also includes water, earth, and how everything is in balance with one another. These are the things that can help us on our journey, so learning about them is vital because a lack of knowledge can make nature a foe rather than a friend.

Chapter Seven

In the beginning, God created both heaven and Earth, and both have been used masterfully over time for the very purpose of honoring God. Also, heaven, Earth, and God are never-ending and will be here forever to fulfill His purpose, and those that serve God will always be protected.

Chapter Eight

The great path can be difficult for many. However, this is because people hate what is good and love their evil thoughts, desires, and material possessions. So while on Earth, think on and do what is right and what is good. When meeting those who do evil in the world, approach them with gentleness and self-control. Try to guide them to the right path with gentleness and without force. If you do that, they will be responsible for their own fate, for you have done what you can. As for yourself? Stay on the path as always.

Chapter Nine

Again, live and be without desires of your own; do not be concerned with what you want, but with what God wants. Do not get caught up with greed, material possessions, bragging, and boasting about what you have, only to eventually lose what you have acquired. Remember that there are many things that can distract you from the right path, so avoid them, for they cannot help you. Instead, always focus on the right path, for this is the true road to take.

Chapter Ten

When you live without your own desires for material goods and just focus on God and oneness of the path, you are on the right and great path. The way to do this is to first be child-like in innocence, just be happy to be, and give without expecting something back. Develop a spirit like a joyous child picking a flower for his mother or handing a tool to his father. Be slow to judge others, remembering the balance of love and law and looking at it from their point of view. Do your best and teach others, but don't be a know-it-all. After all, we learn from each other.

Chapter Eleven

There is so much information available that can help or hurt us. Do not clutter your brain with useless things that can hurt you and take you off the great path. Instead, keep an open and receptive mind to those things that can enhance your life path and spiritual journey, and hold tight to the wisdom you acquire along the way.

Chapter Twelve

There are so many people on Earth who distract themselves with unimportant things they can never get enough of. They see too much, they hear too much, they experience too much, they gather too much, and this excess takes them off the right path. Remember, so many of the material possessions or pleasurable things before us can take us off the eternal path of getting to heaven, which, besides serving God, is the key goal of life. So be careful how you spend your time, for even though the physical body always dies, it is the spirit that lives on forever.

Chapter Thirteen

As you follow the great path, the best way to live your life is by having no desires of your own, but by being one with your spiritual journey and by becoming a humble servant to others. This will keep you grounded on the road God has set before you. If you fully serve others, you will also become less likely to be ambushed with criticism regardless of whether you are rich or poor or your status in life changes. So be at peace with yourself as a servant, for if you help the world by helping others, the world will respond.

Chapter Fourteen

What is the right path to follow? In life, the great path to take is a spiritual one. It is a journey that is not described easily. There is oneness and depth to it, but it is also shapeless and colorless. The path itself guides and helps those who follow it, and it exists from the beginning to the end. In fact, the great spiritual path cannot be seen, heard, or touched, and yet, when looking for it, when listening for it, and when reaching for it, it fills all the senses and our soul. It is a path that has not changed from the beginning of time, and therefore, from the beginning to the end, the great path is embodied by the spirit itself.

Chapter Fifteen

Luckily, the great path contains wise men who can guide us on our way and leaders who have incorporated the word and spirit to help others. So learn from these teachers who have mastered the path. They have carefully crafted and developed the traits needed to experience the path in a wise and profound way. They moved on their journey carefully and with caution, avoiding getting sidetracked with the pitfalls that could take them off course. They were receptive to people's needs, and they took unclear teaching and made it clear to everyone, all without the desire for personal gain. So follow these wise leaders, for they will help keep you on the path.

Chapter Sixteen

When presented with many roads to take, always be receptive to the great path that will lead you to eternal life in heaven. This is accomplished when we focus on the true spiritual path instead of our own personal desires and wishes, and when we become a servant to others. The right path encompasses many things: there will be times to be quiet in thought and reflection, and others times when we should be actively planting the seed of the great path in others. So do much with the little you have to help others and grow the harvest, for when this happens, God will be honored, and you will be rewarded.

Chapter Seventeen

Many people are encountered on the path, and they will come and go. Yet much can be accomplished when we get along with others and strive to help each other through teamwork. How? We build relationships when we are sincere and careful with our words. We also build goodwill with others when we take little credit for ourselves and let everyone involved know that goals were reached because of a team effort. Remember, the path has been around for centuries, loved and praised by the wise, but hated and rejected by others. But let's make the path work for those who desire to take the right road to peace, and together, we can share in its abundance.

Chapter Eighteen

During this life, you will come across false teachers who claim they know the way and use their foolish intellect to take advantage of others. Their way may appear better on the surface, but it only leads to chaos and loss of compassion for others. That's why it's important that true followers of the great path defend its virtue and share it with others so the people won't take the wrong road and be destroyed by these false prophets.

Chapter Nineteen

See the path in its purest form, and follow it. Protect your heart and give love, but also be wary of false teachers and false morality. Beware of those who claim higher wisdom but who actually have false piety and use false giving to impress others. Be on guard to those who are greedy and horde riches, only to succumb to robbery themselves. In the end, always remember that it's important to stay on the solid path, which is accomplished by carefully cultivating your heart.

Chapter Twenty

The great path requires sacrifice and time. It can't just be learned in a classroom; it has to be applied and experienced in everyday life. Consider the dedication involved: While others enjoy treasures and material possessions, I am seemingly alone and tired of going everywhere without a true home in my effort to help others. While other people seem so happy and noticed with many earthly goals and possessions, I often feel ignored. Yet, while I feel different than others, and I may not understand why this is, I know that I am rooted in the path for my benefit, and that brings me joy.

Chapter Twenty-One

When fully discovered, the great spiritual path is so incredible that it cannot be described. It is beyond description and may even seem obscure to some, but it is very real. It is filled with a vastness of knowledge and wisdom for all who follow and are driven by faith and belief. Yes, it is the good and right path that has been here forever, since the beginning of time. It is here to help you, so always follow it.

Chapter Twenty-Two

The great path is perfect and complete when followed. It has amazing beauty in its simplicity, and has all the answers for those that seek to follow it. Since the great path is perfect, it does not have to force its way, brag about what it does, or become contentious. It is without personal desire and seeks to serve others. This is the right path to be on and the path you should follow.

Chapter Twenty-Three

First, you must decide which road to take. Two paths will appear before you, but only one path is the right path to follow. The good news is, once you are on the right path, people will trust you. But take heed, for you cannot change everything and create continuity by yourself. God is in control, and things change. Heaven and Earth can either stop the rain or bring a downpour, or the winds can blow with gale-force or be still. So instead, focus on your own path until you and the path almost become one and the same, and then you can contribute your part to make a true difference.

Chapter Twenty-Four

Wise men know that there is only one great path to follow. They know that following a road other than the great path is the wrong way to go. Other directions may appear to point to a happier way, but it only feeds the ego. Because the wrong way brings pleasures that are temporary, they are disliked by all who seek the truth. Wise followers stay on the right path, keep things in perspective, stay balanced, and don't stray from the great way that leads them. They also keep a low profile, stay humble, and avoid bragging and confrontation. This is the path to follow.

Chapter Twenty-Five

God has created great things. Among the greatest are people, the earth, heaven, and the great spiritual path. They intertwine together on the journey of life. It begins with God and his great spiritual path in heaven. This spiritual path then seeps down from God to heaven, then from heaven to Earth, and from Earth to His people, and His people know Him and follow. The great spiritual path was the beginning, and it continues on as the greatest path to follow.

Chapter Twenty-Six

Life is not easy. Difficulties and heavy burdens will appear, but you need to stay focused. Why? Because God will not give you more than you can handle, and it's important to concentrate on what has to be done now and the tasks ahead. Without focus on the path, the very foundation you have built for yourself and your family can be lost, as well as the ability to guide others on their own journey. Since this would be the wrong road to take, always keep your eyes on the great path.

Chapter Twenty-Seven

You can change someone's life by guiding them to the great spiritual path, and it's vitally important to do so. Why? Because the benefits are immeasurable, it leads to an eternal life, and because being a servant to others is among God's greatest call to his people. However, guiding others should be done with great love and by showing each person the value they have as people and what they have to give, which is an abundance of love from deep within their hearts. It is not done by fault-finding or criticizing or in ways that create stress. Therefore, remember that helping others should always be done with gentle guiding and planting the seed of giving and sharing love, and by keeping in mind that those on the great spiritual path should help those who are not.

Chapter Twenty-Eight

When following the great path, we need to strive for balance. This means that there will be times to be strong and times to be gentle. There will be times to be open to others without judgment, but times to be cautious and wary. So listen to God and be one with the great spiritual path, for when you do, the path will embrace you, comfort you, and carry you. When you are one with the path, you become whole. In the end, God will always give you understanding, so again, listen to what I say, stay on the path, and your way will be abundant and fill all your needs.

Chapter Twenty-Nine

How should you live your life? Start by realizing that there is no need to try and rule the world. You do not need earthly greed and power. Attempts to acquire excessive possessions will make you look overbearing. In fact, greedy manipulating will always bring failure on different levels. Always remember this real truth: Material possessions are fleeting and don't bring real happiness. Instead, stick to the great spiritual path even though it is not always easy because as you already know, sometimes things go right, and sometimes things go wrong. Not getting sidetracked by obstacles and the things you don't need will bring a just reward.

Chapter Thirty

Staying on the great path helps to avoid prolonged confrontation and war because when you go to battle against other people, you tend to dig your own grave. Sometimes we want to beat down those who oppose us even when it is not important. One way to avoid this is to stop bragging, forcing, and demanding your way through life. This is clearly the wrong path to take. Rather, treat people with respect, hear their point of view, and learn quickly so you can stop any negative actions. Finally, while itis good to achieve in life, be humble in doing so, and it will be well received.

Chapter Thirty-One

Make your position with others one of peace and not war whenever you can, and only use weapons as a last resort. If you have to use them, take no joy in it. Only those that like to kill are happy to bring them out and use their force against other people, and because of this, no one trusts them. This is because it is often the regular people who are left to shed tears over burying their own when rulers above them want to go to war. So always remember this: when it comes to weapons, those on the wise path rarely use them.

Chapter Thirty-Two

Follow the path with no fear, and don't be misled by those that say you need a big name or title to be special. Many of these same people on the wrong path will be weeded out and discarded, unable to cope or make adjustments to find their way, and they will have no problem causing divisions among you. But those who stay on the guidelines of the path avoid danger. They will live bravely, with no fear, and are never misled. There is a special balance between heaven and Earth that you must follow, and God in heaven will open up to support you if you stay on the right path.

Chapter Thirty-Three

Be wise and observant. If you do not envy others, you are rich. If you truly understand others, you are intelligent. If you truly understand yourself, you are wise. To overcome both yourself and others is spiritual power. If you combine energy, passion, and great spiritual power, and stay on the great path God has laid out for you, nothing can hold you back, and you will live forever.

Chapter Thirty-Four

The great path from God can never be stopped and is yours to follow. You may get temporarily sidetracked or slowed in your journey, but stop resisting and turn back to the spiritual path, and it will reveal its greatness. Like a flood, the great path cannot be stopped, helps to clothe and feed those in need, and guides and dresses people on their way with kindness, humbleness, and compassion.

Chapter Thirty-Five

The spiritual path is challenging, and temptation is all around, including things like excessive wine and food that leads one to gluttony. There are also other sinful desires and wrongful pleasures that distract people from following the right spiritual path and can only lead to emptiness. So always remember that the right path is the heavenly spirit in action, guiding you along the way, and is there for the taking. So, my friend, let me say this: Hold onto the great path on your journey, and you will forever rest in peace.

Chapter Thirty-Six

When you follow the great spiritual path, you become a new you, so do it now. Replace the old you on the inside, and empty out the things you do not need. Fill your heart, mind, and soul with the new things of your spiritual path. This can be accomplished by overcoming your resistance to change, and by developing your soft and tender side. When you do this, you will realize that peace and gentleness will overcome the aggressiveness and fighting that can only lead to falling off the path. Instead, become new and one with the spirit, and go forward on the path.

Chapter Thirty-Seven

To be a true leader, we must embrace the spiritual path. We must also realize that the path reflects our inner being and not just what we do in our lives. Yes, what we do is important, but even more so is our inner spiritual being, which is developed from a reflective and meditative prayer life. So develop this true and vital spiritual life that encompasses every moment and reflects the deep inner being. Also, make sure the inner changes are honest and done without being forced or in a false way, but rather in a way that reflects a pure heart. Always remember this: when we follow the great spiritual path, heaven will be pleased.

Chapter Thirty-Eight

One of the fastest ways a leader can win over the people is to be authentic and genuine. Why? It's because people can often sense fake, superficial morality, and will see through false motives. So a leader must be real to the deepest niches of his heart. He must get to know and understand himself inside and out. He must put aside pretending to be nice, get rid of false airs if they are present, and pursue the true goodness and spirituality of a pure heart. He must not lead with manipulative or selfish reasons because anger will arise if he pretends to have a person's best interests in mind and does not. Anger will rise again if he pretends to be loyal and sincere to someone but does not keep his word. So reach down to your soul and treat people with kindness, sincerity, and compassion on your journey.

Chapter Thirty-Nine

Have you ever thought about why God's spiritual path is important on Earth? Without it, people would stumble, there would be even less peace, the best rulers would be ineffective, and the best of things would vanish. There would be a spiritual void and great emptiness in the hearts of His people. Besides, God does not want divisions among His people, but rather oneness on a path he will make clear to see. The peace and spirit of the path come to fill the voids and lead to wholeness and happiness. Therefore, if you are humble, can avoid distractions, can live without your own personal desires, and can focus on God, then the greatness of the path will be revealed to you.

Chapter Forty

Essentially, everyone is on a path. But there is only one right path: the great path from above that guides our way. So if you leave the wrong path that you are on, and get back on course with the great and true path, your burden will be lighter. Additionally, you also demonstrate your wisdom and honor God by coming back to the right spiritual path, moving yourself from someone who is discounted and forgotten, to a person who becomes of value to others.

Chapter Forty-One

Following the great spiritual path is not easy. It is criticized and laughed at by some. These are the people who don't understand it at all. Those who are more neutral hear the good news and sometimes follow it for a short time before failing. However, members of the third group are superior students who hear the path and follow it. These are students who make the long and tedious sacrifice, and who often stand alone for that which is right. So sadly, while the good news that the path represents is either hard to grasp or rejected by some, for those who do understand, explore, and follow the right path in a changing world, there will be joy, for they will be able to reach the highest pinnacle of their true self and honor God.

Chapter Forty-Two

Life is a balance of gain and loss. True, sometimes to gain is good and to lose is bad, but the opposite can also be true. For instance, we can gain a material possession that may distract us from what we should actually be doing, while we may lose a bad habit, which benefits us. So we must understand the give-and-take or yin and yang of life that leads to harmony along the great path. This means staying away from hurtful desires, impulsive force, or demanding a way that leads to your demise. To do that, always follow the flow of the great path.

Chapter Forty-Three

As you journey along the great path on Earth, you will encounter opposition and strife and meet the ways of the world that can harm you and take you off the great path. However, you no longer belong to the world, so instead of being discouraged, meet these challenges and obstacles with the gentleness and persistence of doing what God has called you to do. Yes, let the spiritual path move you forward in a positive way, overflowing with love for others, and without personal desire of your own, other than the desire to overcome all opposition with love.

Chapter Forty-Four

Material possessions mean little on the great spiritual path. In fact, the intense desire to accumulate and possess wealth or material objects can come back to haunt you. Everyone needs some of these things to function, of course; but those on the right path know when their needs are met and when they have enough. It is this balance between excess and greed and having just enough to live on that becomes an important lesson to learn on your journey.

Chapter Forty-Five

The great path is revealed to those who really believe, while others reject it. Some may feel that it may not provide the grand fun they want, and those who are uninformed even see it as contradictory. However, the real truth is that the road to destruction is wide and many will take that way, while the great path is narrow and only a few will chose it. Yes, the journey is not easy, but it does not require perfection, but rather the clarity to see the bigger picture and making a choice to become one with the great spiritual path. When this is accomplished, it will ultimately lead to great peace.

Chapter Forty-Six

Why go to war with other countries and other people? Don't you see the current suffering many people are going through, dealing with things you may not even realize? So enough is enough; stop the greed, stop the anger, stop the fighting, and be content with what you have. Get back on the great spiritual path, and when you do, you will have true peace and contentment.

Chapter Forty-Seven

Does it take higher education like a doctorate or pastoral degree to follow the great path? No. Does it require sitting in a classroom or at a seminary for years to take the journey of the great path? No. While all these things may have their place, God inherently writes the truth into the hearts of men. No formal or special education is needed to follow the spiritual path to get to heaven, and in fact, sometimes the more education and experience one has means that less is known! Why? Because God reveals truth to those who really follow the great path regardless of titles or formal education, and the wisest of men learn this quickly.

Chapter Forty-Eight

While formal education is not required to follow the great path, as we know, what will be required is a thirst for knowledge. To do this, you must first let go of the old worldly things you were taught that can actually hurt you and are no longer needed, replacing them with new knowledge that keeps you on the right path. When this happens, you can ultimately reach a level of self-actualization and peace. It also means letting go of manipulating ways, the desire for personal gain, and all the things of the world that distract you and take you off course. Now, does it really matter if you are greedy or treat others badly for personal gain? Yes, it does. Remember it with this question: What good would it do to gain all the things that the earthy world has to offer, but lose your soul?

Chapter Forty-Nine

Life is tough for all of us, so be gentle with others. Remember, everyone is trying to do what they think is best at that moment for themselves, but all people make mistakes and sometimes eagerly rush into them without thinking or caring about the consequences. So live with compassion and forgiveness for others. In fact, a good way to protect yourself is to remember not to expect too much from people, but be elated when they do right so you won't be disappointed. Remember, God loves unconditionally—so should you.

Chapter Fifty

So many people are distracted away from the great spiritual path and led down the road to destruction by the pleasures of life along the way: wine, women, sex, gluttony, greed, and many others. Always remember, the great path provides real and sustaining joy, happiness, and pleasure. So stay on the one true path that gives real life and passion, and use cautious intelligence when false pleasures are presented to you. It is the great path that leads to true happiness, and true happiness leads to God.

Chapter Fifty-One

In life, you are not forced to follow the great path; it is presented to you without demands and threats. In fact, you are given free will to follow any path you choose, but choose carefully, my friend, because the path you pick can either punish you or protect you. In other words, a wise choice can help raise you up to become what you were meant to be, while a bad choice can literally destroy you. So what will you decide? The smart choice is the wise and great spiritual path, which guides us and gives meaning and quality to life.

Chapter Fifty-Two

Again, as your journey begins, keep your focus on the great path. It is not just the trappings of wealth or luxury that can take you off course, but even the everyday things of this life that can take you off the right path. However, if you stay true to the teachings of the true path until you die, you will harvest much fruit along the way. Of course, you must be flexible and take time for the small things that give life meaning, but be cautious or you will be thrown off course. So in the end, you must be, as they say, "gentle as a dove, but wary as a serpent" so you can always stay close to the wise and great path.

Chapter Fifty-Three

As we know, the right path can be tough for some to follow as they are distracted by the things of this life like wine, women, and song. These are the same people that often try to the take shortcuts in life or indulge in other seemingly pleasurable roads that lead to either nowhere or destruction, and who really and selfishly only care about themselves. This is obviously not the right path to take. What should you do? The true and great path requires focus, sacrifice, and wisdom.

Chapter Fifty-Four

The true path has been around forever, from generation to generation, so be careful to not let this great spiritual path slip from your grip. Instead, cling tightly to it because it determines everything in your life and your very destiny. Also, when you follow the right way, you become a model for all those that come after you. So worship the spiritual path and the God who gave it to you, and pass it on to all you encounter, including your family, friends, the country, and the world. By doing so, you help others find the great path.

Chapter Fifty-Five

Let me say it again: holding tight to the right path in life creates lasting spiritual power and harmony. The self-control and sacrifice you develop along the way illuminates and nourishes life, so others will want the same peace you have. They will want to take the same path that you have taken, for it will help them grow into individuals who develop respected traits that most honorable people desire, including moral integrity, good character, and fairness, along with being someone who is above attack when examined by fair-minded people. However, it is a choice, as the right path leads to life, while following the wrong path leads to death.

Chapter Fifty-Six

Let's do our best to get along with everyone, and in this way, we can achieve peace by being peacemakers ourselves. You see, every person is responsible for every idle word they speak, and so what we say can make a situation better or worse. Therefore, whenever possible, speak in a manner that promotes goodwill and togetherness, not anger. In fact, at times, a person can benefit from the non-action of silence. Why? Because even if you are right and others do not know what they are saying, they will resent you for trying to prove them wrong. So let oneness be your goal whenever possible, and the world will respond and take notice.

Chapter Fifty-Seven

Peace in the world can be a difficult thing to find. Why? This often happens because there is a poor interpretation of words and laws that leads to anger and rebellion in the people. Also, the world is bogged down by too many laws, too many guns, and too much cleverness and deception by those who try to take advantage of other people. So how can peace and good will be achieved? They are created when we don't force our way through life with impure motives. It happens when we treat people with fairness and respect, and it happens when we sincerely help each other make good choices. When we do these uplifting things, we can achieve the peace and serenity we desire.

Chapter Fifty-Eight

One of the problems many leaders have is the unnecessary criticism of others to attempt to motivate them for their own personal gain. Sometimes these leaders use micromanaging and fault-finding as a way to accomplish this. However, this is the wrong way to go because what can you accomplish when you make people feel bad about themselves? Instead, more can be achieved if we let people be who they are while being gentle in our correction. When a leader can relax and reflect on how he treats people, he will come to realize that he can create goodwill by correcting and teaching in a gentle way that inspires growth. So leaders should find and share with their people what they are doing right at various times, and then occasional correction will be better received.

Chapter Fifty-Nine

Every leader has various resources at hand to help the people. However, how he uses these materials, goods, and money in his possession is how he will be viewed. Therefore, the wise leader first begins by planting the roots of the right path and its wisdom in place to create goodwill. In doing so, he creates trust. Next, the effective, welcomed leader carefully studies how to divide these resources fairly. It will be his wise judgment and perceived fairness with these valuable resources that will instill confidence in the people and help creates prosperity for all involved. So if you want to lead, know what you can give to your people, and distribute it wisely.

Chapter Sixty

Every great leader is guided by wisdom. Wisdom is that inner knowledge that guides what we do, and it is wisdom that can pull us toward good decisions and repel us away from bad ones. Wise decisions make the burdens in life lighter and can lead to a fruitful future. Those leaders that use wisdom every day create a path where evil is lessened and true harm will not come. So keep this in mind: wisdom is simply the ability of using experience, knowledge, and good judgment to come to a conclusion, and it is always important for every decision-maker to use wisdom.

Chapter Sixty-One

Helping others is among our greatest gifts. We simply need each other, and a life of service to others makes us stronger. Why? Because it can be difficult to get things done by yourself, but imagine what you can accomplish and the unity created by coming together rather than trying to do it on your own. How can we achieve this unity? It begins by thinking of others before ourselves and by being a true servant to all, with nobody being better than anyone else. When we help others, it creates a ripple of success for all. So remember that people who work together will prosper, and there will be much gain when people come together and are servants to each other.

Chapter Sixty-Two

Many take different roads to find fulfillment and peace, but true peace can only be found by taking the great path, for it is priceless. Even the highest of kings with all of their riches cannot buy the true path. The great path is known for its worth, but free to follow. What joys await those who make the sacrifice and develop oneness with this way of faith, and words and deeds and kindness and compassion. In the end, this true path has worth because it is without personal desire and serves to benefit God, which benefits us all.

Chapter Sixty-Three

No matter our path, problems will come up. When they do, act quickly and do not delay. If you have a dispute with someone, settle your differences as soon as possible. In fact, you should treat each difficult situation as a project that must be dealt with now. Begin by making an honest and sincere evaluation of the matter, and always respond to any anger or hate with kindness and compassion whenever possible. In doing so, you can correct any trouble before it gets too big, and when problems are kept small and in perspective, it helps to remove the obstacles you may encounter on the great path.

Chapter Sixty-Four

Like I said before, the best way to finish projects is to start early and without delay. Too many people wait until the last minute to begin work, when the best way is to methodically push forward at a steady pace and without rushing. That's because hurrying through a project often leads to carelessness, poor quality, and sometimes failure. However, if one works carefully from beginning to end, it often leads to success. We should also get along well with others, and the wise leader accomplishes this by putting his desires aside and learning the heart of the people. He then works next to them as a servant, not as a boss, which wins their respect and creates unity and success.

Chapter Sixty-Five

What is the wrong path, and what is the right path? The wrong path is wide and filled with many people who are dishonest and immoral. Eventually, their lying, cheating, and deceit will catch up with them. If you are wise, you will know that this is the wrong road to take. Then what is the right road? The great path is narrow and requires character and integrity. This begs the question: What is character and integrity? They mean having a strong moral compass built on honesty and fairness, doing the right thing when nobody is looking, saying what you mean, not gossiping, and always promoting truth and love. In the end, if you have character and integrity built on honesty and clarity, and can avoid just telling people what they want to hear, then the people will follow you. You will then be someone who can help and guide others on their own journey along the great path.

Chapter Sixty-Six

Being humble is among the most important traits a leader can have. He does not brag or boast, but simply approaches every project with calm focus and fairness. He wants the best for his people and cares about them, and because he projects humbleness, the people view him fairly and he becomes like one of them, rather than as an oppressive dictator. In fact, consider the volume of the seas combined; this equates to the vastness of support a ruler will get from the people who clamor for this type of heartfelt leadership. In fact, not only will followers quickly accept the humble, fair leader, they will be enthusiastic to follow him.

Chapter Sixty-Seven

How should we live? The great spiritual path reveals the way you should live your life. First, it involves living with no desire for yourself, only for God. It means happily living within the means God gives you. It means being humble and not thinking of yourself as better than others or by claiming superiority or elevated brilliance. It is by realizing that there is always more to learn, and that on the inside, we are all the same. It means remembering that life is not really worth living if you do not treat others with empathy, compassion, and love. So rely on heaven along every step of the path, and the compassion you share will be rewarded with compassion.

Chapter Sixty-Eight

The time will come when you will be attacked in a variety of ways. What should you do? During these times, be balanced and keep your composure and wits about you. In other words, try to stay calm and listen. The best approach to take in these situations is to defuse this anger whenever possible, keeping in mind that the best defense is one where further attack or war is not needed, and no foolish risks are taken. In fact, as a counterattack, treat these people with great respect. Try to win them over by appealing to their fairness and their ability to do the right thing, and try to catch them doing something right that you can praise them on. Getting them to move at least a little bit to your side of a discussion can help end the conflict. When you can achieve this, heaven will rejoice.

Chapter Sixty-Nine

When it is hard to get along with someone, it is sometimes wise to find middle ground. How? First, quickly evaluate all circumstances in dealing with the other person. Know when to give ground in a debate or conflict, or as the card-playing adage goes, "know when to hold 'em, know when to fold 'em." Why? You may be easily able to win a debate or argument, but how will the other person feel? You may be right about a subject, but destroy good will. So always keep your "weapons" hidden if possible, know what points you can agree on, and try to accomplish as much as possible without a fight. However, never compromise your values on the great path. Additionally, keep a proper respect for all people and opponents, and don't take anyone for granted, because if you do, it could mean defeat, so try to get along with everyone whenever possible.

Chapter Seventy

Why is the great path so important? Because it will change the life of those who follow it. Yet, there are many who do not follow the great path or practice its teachings. They are consumed with their own personal desires, so they end up on the wide road to destruction. These people need to understand that these laws of wisdom all come together with the oneness of the path to help them. In fact, if all people were really able to instinctively understand the true blessings and abundant life attached to taking the great path, then my guidance would not be needed. However, since people remain stubborn and choose personal gain over wisdom, these teachings remain important, with hope that many will finally see the light.

Chapter Seventy-One

It certainly is a great thing to acquire knowledge and to use this wisdom and information to help others. However, it's also important to share information in a humble way that creates a receptive audience. In fact, when you admit you don't know everything, you earn respect. Remember, know-it-alls are annoying, so if you lack information about a subject, say so. If you are wrong about something, admit it. It comes down to this: not knowing the facts about something but thinking you do is both arrogance and a form of illness. Being humble and being honest about what you know and what you don't know means being respected.

Chapter Seventy-Two

Sadly, an inferiority complex can damage our lives, and it takes so little for that to happen. It often begins with negative emotions that usually arise out of fear, and then attack and damage our self-esteem. Then, frustrated because we don't know how to change ourselves, we begin to attack others. Some of these attacks include trying to control others, getting into their business to bring them down, and thinking that it will help us feel better about ourselves. These methods almost always fail. Therefore, the right path to take is letting go of fear, building others up, and learning how we can respect ourselves so we can respect others. In this way, we win people over when we let go of the desire to control them and treat them as we would want to be treated.

Chapter Seventy-Three

The great path to heaven can be narrow. Why? Because the right path takes both courage and bravery to follow it while avoiding foolishness at the same time. Those who take silly risks and make bad choices end up on the well-traveled road to destruction. Don't let this happen to you; instead, use the many resources and tools heaven has to offer. This happens when we get on the true path, set goals, limit worrying, and try to relax and live in the moment. Remember, we don't have to understand everything or all the mysterious ways of God, as even great leaders don't understand everything about heaven and its ways. However, we can be content by moving forward on the right path and combining courage, wisdom, intelligence, and faith to help us find our way and keep us going in the right direction.

Chapter Seventy-Four

For those who can hear, listen to this wise advice: Anger and fear rarely make a situation better, and in fact, can turn the most well-intentioned conversation into a bitter argument not soon forgotten. Why? While the actual words can hurt, they may not be remembered over time. However, what people will remember is how you say things, your tone of voice, and your body language. Additionally, even if someone goes along with another person's ranting and raving, eventually, resentment sets in. In fact, people who instill fear to control others will be revolted against and met with hate. So why use it when it can only harm? Instead, stay away from the wrong path of anger, idle threats, and fear as negotiation tools that always backfire, and instead choose the wise communication tools of love and peace whenever possible. This is following the great path.

Chapter Seventy-Five

Sadly, greed can destroy the best of friends. In life, we want to believe that we are surrounded by kind and generous people, but ultimately, we come across people who are only out for themselves. Some are obsessed with greed regardless of who gets hurt, and to make matters worse, they refuse to share what they have to help others. Naturally, this selfishness is often met with anger by those who oppose them. For example, imagine a country where the ruler imposes high taxes while his people starve. In this situation, the people will not fear this so-called leader; they will first have contempt, and then revolt. So whether coming across an exalted ruler or working peasant, treat everyone with kindness and generosity, and think of others before yourself so you can be at peace. This is the right path to take.

Chapter Seventy-Six

Life is a balance between good times and bad times. By the time we become adults, we have endured our fair of share of hardships, and if we haven't, they are likely on the way. When they come, they can impact the way we live our lives and can create dysfunction. During these difficult times, they can also have a negative impact on our conscious and unconscious mind. In fact, if enough damage has been done, we can become adults that walk around being harsh, cold, bitter, and critical, thus creating a person so damaged, we can become unwavering and cynical in both our thinking and our actions. So what is the alternative? Live your life as a good-natured child would. This would be a child that is accepting of others, soft-hearted, open-minded, and gentle—a child who is open to new ideas, tries to bring people together, and is open to compromise and caring. Remember, when seeking true happiness, try to find your inner child.

Chapter Seventy-Seven

Are you a person who helps others or cheats them? Unfortunately, the world is filled with those people who become more and more greedy for money and material things. In fact, not only don't they help the poor, but they take advantage of them as well. This is obviously the wrong path to take in life. Instead, those who are able to help people should do so. So give what you can and cheerfully provide for the poor and those in need. This selfless and humble giving puts you on the right path here on Earth, and this leads to heaven.

Chapter Seventy-Eight

Many times in life, rocks, arrows, and other insults are thrown our way. Obstacles are all around us, and eventually, they may even become the boulders that block our path. If we stray from the right way and accept this corruption in our lives, it becomes our master. We then become heavy laden with worry, weakness, and feelings of being overwhelmed. However, consider water, which takes on the shape of the container it fills. With persistence, water can erode the rock over time with gentle pressure. Remember this as you focus on your goals and your path. If you are like water, you will persistently move forward, eroding or moving around obstacles until you become a success and reach your destiny.

Chapter Seventy-Nine

At times, we can find ourselves encountering people who are angry or jealous and don't want the best for us. These schemers may even interfere with our business and hold grudges over the slightest of perceived injustices. Eventually, however, these same people lose credibility and are no longer trusted because their way of treating good citizens is not soon forgotten. Obviously, this is not the right way. Instead, my friend, choose a path where you treat people with kindness and compassion and where disputes are settled quickly. Additionally, always try to keep your promises, which reflects strong integrity. This will help keep you on the great path.

Chapter Eighty

As much as possible, protect yourself and stay out of quarrels. Be glad with a precious, simple way of living, and don't forget what is really important, which is to find great value and joy in life. Next, be at peace with your neighbor and work harmoniously together. Finally, give of yourself and what you have in terms of food, shelter, and clothes.

Chapter Eighty-One

The beauty of the great path is its simplicity. You don't need the complexity of examination or higher education to follow it, because human understanding is mere foolishness to God. In fact, it is often the uneducated and those that learn by experience who have the best understanding of the path. These people are often simple in speech and don't argue with others. They also know that we have a giving God who will help us prosper when we go the right way. So stay on the great path, which will keep you from harm and lead you to heaven.

About the Author

Kevin M. Thomas is an award-winning author of titles like, *Tao Te Ching De-Coded* and *Why Daughters Need Their Dads*, and has a varied background in medicine, alternative health, counseling, religion, and mind-body healing. Kevin is passionate about promoting and delivering positive change to any person, and he strives to affect personal growth in individuals via mind-body-spirit research and application. Finally, he considers his relationship with God and his unconditional love for his children, Isiah, Caroline, Kimberly, and Cheyenne, as his greatest treasures.

The Great Path

The Great Path is a modern interpretation of the *Tao Te Ching*, the second-most translated book in the world, next to the Bible. The *Tao Te Ching* in itself is a book of wisdom and a guide to finding the right path in life—a path that involves simplicity, inner peace, passion, and compassion, focusing on what is important along the journey. Additionally, this book can help you discover your true purpose in life, and often serves as the catalyst to help someone find the great path lurking within all our souls.

KETNA PUBLISHING: Kevin Thomas and Erik Naugle make up KETNA Publishing, a small, hometown publisher located in mid-Michigan. Their goal is to deliver high-quality information into the hands of the people so they can positively change their lives via body, mind, and spirit application. You can contact KETNA Publishing at kt123trailblazer@gmail.com or grobthom@aol.com or write to KETNA Publishing, P.O. Box 90861, Burton, Michigan, 48509.

www.ingramcontent.com/pod-product-compliance
Lightning Source LLC
Chambersburg PA
CBHW070544300426
44113CB00011B/1788